SSAT/ISEE Core Vocabulary

By

James Jones

Introduction

An extensive vocabulary is one of the most important skills required for SSAT/ISEE success. Unfortunately, it is also one of the most difficult skills to master, as getting young kids to memorize hundreds of words is easier said than done!

One of the best ways to learn new words is to practice using vocabulary in different contexts such as:

- Synonyms
- Antonyms
- Spellings
- Fill in Blanks
- Odd one Out
- Missing Letters

This book contains 100 varied and interesting exercises enabling kids to learn new words and consolidate their learning quickly and efficiently.
Each exercise contains 20 or more different words that have appeared in the SSAT/ISEE (Lower/Middle) tests in recent past.

Some of the exercises are designed to enable kids to work with *groups of words* with similar/opposite meanings, enabling quicker absorption of whole sets of new words.

Learning how to spell correctly aides in learning new words and helps with retaining their meaning.

This book has multiple exercises to test vocabulary combined with spellings.

Answers to all exercises are provided at the end of the book.

A child should try to do 2 or 3 exercises every day and make note of any new words to be revised later.

Table of Contents

1. Antonyms

Instruction: Complete the antonym of the word in bold.

1. **break**   m ___ ___ d

2. **friend**   f ___ ___

3. **like**   d ___ ___ ___ ___ ___ e

4. **smile**   f ___ ___ ___ n

5. **stale**   f ___ ___ ___ h

6. **safe**   d ___ ___ ___ ___ ___ ___ ___ s

7. **begin**   f ___ ___ ___ ___ h

8. **past**   f ___ ___ ___ ___ e

9. **cry**   l ___ ___ ___ h

10. **difficult**   e ___ ___ y

11. **better**   w ___ ___ ___ e

12. **famous**   u n ___ ___ ___ ___ n

13. **alive**   d ___ ___ d

14. **stay**   l e ___ ___ e

15. **stable**   u n ___ ___ ___ ___ ___ e

16. **start**   e ___ d

17. **believe**   d o ___ ___ t

18. **pale**   c o ___ ___ ___ ___ ___ u l

19. **colossal**   t ___ ___ y

20. **different**   s ___ ___ e

2. Happy or Sad

Instruction: Write the matching synonyms from the Word Bank underneath the words in bold.
(Two words have been done for you)

Word Bank

cheery	blue	grinning	woeful	beaming
woebegone	glum	jolly	gleeful	buoyant
merry	forlorn	contented	sunny	upbeat
down	depressed	miserable	sorrowful	gloomy

Happy	**Sad**
cheery	*blue*

3. Synonyms

Instruction: Find the word that is closest in meaning to the word in bold. Cross it out.

1.	**absent**	far	true	present	away
2.	**abundant**	copious	scarce	few	declining
3.	**best**	last	evil	worst	greatest
4.	**bent**	warped	straight	right	left
5.	**accept**	forgive	receive	commence	lie
6.	**admit**	conceal	live	disclose	deny
7.	**clear**	opaque	transparent	dark	clean
8.	**calm**	wild	tranquil	care	cook
9.	**kind**	ugly	cruel	friendly	harsh
10.	**cautious**	boring	warm	careful	blend
11.	**forget**	remember	fake	fast	omit
12.	**rectify**	correct	destroy	to build	to command
13.	**paramount**	very important	fake	famous	wide
14.	**tasty**	aesthetic	abundant	delicious	imposing
15.	**enigmatic**	clear	obvious	puzzling	pithy
16.	**cohesion**	shift	climbing	solidarity	independent
17.	**refund**	borrow	take	receive	repay
18.	**domain**	main	area	marketing	internet
19.	**skip**	bypass	notice	insert	introduce
20.	**candid**	anxious	frank	experienced	secretive

4. Yes and No Game

Instructions: Write "Yes" in Column B if the words in Column A are antonyms. If they are NOT antonyms, write "No" then write an antonym for the first word. Several antonyms are possible. *(First two questions have been done for you).*

Column A	Column B
1. **lose – find**	*Yes*
2. **hard – thick**	*No. Antonym of hard is soft*
3. **tall – short**	
4. **wide – narrow**	
5. **flat – level**	
6. **many – few**	
7. **whine – cry**	
8. **round – circular**	
9. **poverty – destitution**	
10. **ahead – behind**	
11. **little – giant**	
12. **catch – apprehend**	
13. **shout – whisper**	
14. **prohibit – protect**	
15. **connect – weld**	
16. **win – lose**	
17. **unhappy – cheerful**	
18. **dull – fun**	
19. **decline – accept**	
20. **rich - opulent**	

5. Strong or Weak

Instruction: Write the matching synonyms from the Word Bank underneath the words in bold.

Word Bank

athletic	powerful	fragile	forceful	sick
tough	redoubtable	rickety	stout	delicate
brawny	fatigued	flimsy	infirm	solid
spent	fit	debilitated	feeble	firm

Strong	**Weak**

6. Synonyms

Instruction: Complete the synonym of the word in bold.

1. **happen**   o c ___ ___ r
2. **reject**   d ___ ___ y
3. **coarse**   r o ___ ___ h
4. **value**   w o ___ ___ h
5. **old**   a ___ ___ ___ ___ n t
6. **quiet**   s___ ___ ___ n t
7. **rug**   c a ___ ___ ___ t
8. **ask**   e ___ ___ ___ ___ r e
9. **writer**   a ___ ___ ___ o r
10. **mix**   b ___ ___ ___ d
11. **freedom**   l ___ ___ ___ ___ t y
12. **boredom**   m o ___ ___ ___ ___ ___ y
13. **place**   i n ___ ___ r t
14. **sweet**   s u ___ ___ r y
15. **small**   t ___ ___ y
16. **sick**   u ___ ___ ___ l l
17. **trick**   d e ___ ___ ___ v e
18. **brave**   c o ___ ___ ___ ___ ___ ___ u s
19. **truthfulness**   h ___ ___ ___ ___ ___ y
20. **maintain**   c ___ ___ ___ ___ ___ ___ ___ e

7. Lots and Few

Instruction: Write the matching synonyms from the Word Bank underneath the words in bold.

Word Bank

plenty	many	lean	meager	several
copious	sparse	rare	scarce	heaps
tons	infrequent	little	abundant	paltry
slight	myriad	dozens	piles	scant

Lots	**Few**

8. Antonyms

Instruction: Find the antonym of the word in bold. Cross it out.

1. **innocent**	interesting	brave	guilty	plain
2. **timid**	bald	bold	popular	evil
3. **simple**	unique	complicated	misleading	brilliant
4. **thrift**	poverty	extravagance	shop	musical
5. **blunt**	sharp	plain	blend	swing
6. **fertile**	gradual	unrefined	sterile	compressed
7. **noisy**	curious	boring	cold	quiet
8. **safe**	sane	dull	reliable	hazardous
9. **polite**	diligent	secure	recent	discourteous
10. **wrong**	mad	complete	accurate	abundant
11. **lethargic**	heavy	neat	easy	energetic
12. **loyal**	unethical	rude	risky	treacherous
13. **answer**	reply	question	borrow	rejoin
14. **aspiration**	desire	reward	thought	aimlessness
15. **push**	play	stop	pull	hit
16. **ally**	friend	neighbor	soldier	enemy
17. **always**	sometimes	together	tomorrow	never
18. **vacant**	certain	occupied	slow	tiresome
19. **famous**	mindful	popular	obscure	adequate
20. **regular**	often	subdued	recent	rare

9. Odd One Out

Instruction: Find which word is the odd one out. Cross it out.

1.	believe	suppose	reject	trust
2.	attempt	test	adjust	try
3.	forgive	achieve	excuse	pardon
4.	adolescent	mature	grown	adult
5.	stray	cat	kitten	feline
6.	apparel	costume	attire	bare
7.	flood	swamp	outpouring	draught
8.	develop	grow	raise	shrink
9.	well	better	nice	awful
10.	chant	sing	sob	hum
11.	divine	atrocious	ghastly	dreadful
12.	above	underneath	below	beneath
13.	smooth	wrinkle	crinkle	crease
14.	once	forever	always	eternally
15.	silence	scream	tranquil	quiet
16.	obese	overweight	chubby	scrawny
17.	soft	rigid	delicate	tender
18.	lively	active	sickly	alive
19.	famished	ravenous	starved	filled
20.	frequent	seldom	often	repeatedly

10. Beautiful and Ugly

Instruction: Write the matching synonyms from the Word Bank underneath the words in bold.

Word Bank

comely	hideous	alluring	exquisite	unsightly
attractive	ghastly	pleasant	enthralling	nasty
repellent	dazzling	stunning	deformed	gorgeous
awful	lovely	grotesque	disgusting	repulsive

Beautiful	**Ugly**

11. Synonym

Instruction: Write the matching synonym from the Word Bank on the blank line.
(The first word had been done for you).

Word Bank

absolve	mediate	valid	traumatic	dilemma
elude	contrast	generate	perception	alternative
mistake	fluctuate	beneficial	mandatory	infamous
scrutiny	sabotage	derive	evaluate	mortify

1. **acquit**   *absolve*
2. **dissimilarity** _____
3. **oscillate** _____
4. **produce** _____
5. **conciliate** _____
6. **distressing** _____
7. **helpful** _____
8. **sound** _____
9. **compulsory** _____
10. **predicament** _____
11. **insight** _____
12. **inspection** _____
13. **evade** _____
14. **notorious** _____
15. **substitute** _____
16. **oversight** _____
17. **appraise** _____
18. **obtain** _____
19. **humiliate** _____
20. **subvert** _____

12. Synonym

Instruction: Find the synonym of the word in bold. Cross it out.

1.	**believe**	tailor	trust	recognize	deny
2.	**greedy**	lovely	voracious	diet	flavored
3.	**happiness**	contagious	leisure	pleasure	playful
4.	**hardworking**	lazy	mean	diligent	deceitful
5.	**refuse**	accept	acknowledge	reject	return
6.	**major**	minor	trivial	little	significant
7.	**hollow**	solid	star	flow	empty
8.	**sweet**	spirit	honored	pleasant	mailed
9.	**brag**	boast	show	perform	applause
10.	**give**	take	get	greed	grant
11.	**quick**	far	slow	deep	fast
12.	**tired**	hire	energy	sleepy	extraordinary
13.	**sleepy**	alert	drowsy	bored	aloof
14.	**neat**	expert	deal	tidy	messy
15.	**soft**	muddy	mushy	menace	marshmallow
16.	**mad**	afar	upset	trial	bespoken
17.	**male**	fragile	female	flare	masculine
18.	**malevolent**	fairy	good	better	malicious
19	**adolescent**	adult	toddler	teenager	adorn
20.	**adult**	spoiled	spare	mature	father

13. Forbid or Permit

Instruction: Write the matching synonyms from the Word Bank underneath the words in bold.

Word Bank

entitle	enjoin	approve	allow	restrain
interdict	ban	grant	outlaw	authorize
preclude	prohibit	veto	block	permit
let	sanction	disallow	empower	proscribe

Forbid	**Permit**

14. Antonym

Instruction: Write the matching antonym from the Word Bank on the blank.

Word Bank

implicit	deficient	climb	inclusive	tranquility
begin	inaccurate	converge	deduct	enthusiastic
flourish	formidable	agitation	immune	diurnal
leave	carnivore	virtuoso	outgoing	protagonist

1. **add** _____

2. **fail** _____

3. **abundant** _____

4. **susceptible** _____

5. **apathetic** _____

6. **diverge** _____

7. **stay** _____

8. **terminate** _____

9. **chaos** _____

10. **herbivore** _____

11. **explicit** _____

12. **nocturnal** _____

13. **exact** _____

14. **powerless** _____

15. **exclusive** _____

16. **antagonist** _____

17. **descend** _____

18. **repose** _____

19. **amateur** _____

20. **introverted** _____

15. Antonyms

Instruction: Complete the antonym of the word in bold.

1. **boastful**   m o ___ ___ ___ t

2. **fragile**   r e ___ ___ ___ ___ ___ n t

3. **clumsy**   g r ___ ___ ___ ___ u l

4. **attract**   r ___ ___ e l

5. **clean-shaven**   b ___ ___ ___ ___ e d

6. **approach**   l e ___ ___ e

7. **introverted**   o ___ ___ ___ ___ ___ ___ g

8. **offer**   a c ___ ___ ___ t

9. **ornate**   p ___ ___ ___ n

10. **poverty**   l ___ ___ ___ ___ y

11. **get**   g ___ ___ e

12. **absent**   p ___ ___ ___ ___ n t

13. **defense**   o f ___ ___ ___ ___ e

14. **improve**   d e ___ ___ ___ ___ ___ ___ ___ t e

15. **stick by**   a b ___ ___ ___ o n

16. **broad**   n a ___ ___ ___ w

17. **risky**   s ___ ___ e

18. **appear**   v ___ ___ ___ s h

19. **allow**   p r ___ ___ ___ ___ t

20. **useful**   u ___ ___ ___ ___ s s

16. Synonyms

Instruction: Find the synonym of the word in bold. Cross it out.

1.	**humble**	modest	illiterate	trying	prone
2.	**loud**	siren	deafening	proud	quiet
3.	**modern**	old-fashioned	contemporary	interesting	daily
4.	**rich**	healthy	wealthy	poor	hearty
5.	**sceptic**	trusting	trustful	try	cynic
6.	**lie**	encourage	truth	stand	untruth
7.	**pail**	dim	dark	bucket	straight
8.	**stay**	go	leave	wait	learn
9.	**down**	upright	cheery	unhappy	delay
10.	**cover**	expose	choose	protect	explain
11.	**intelligent**	quick-witted	dull	dumb	shrink
12.	**tough**	strong	weak	denial	abandon
13.	**alert**	expensive	inattentive	vigilant	stray
14.	**disclosure**	state	revelation	blunt	sentence
15.	**fight**	build	brawl	take	left
16.	**arrange**	ahead	organize	district	attend
17.	**distract**	allow	deny	divert	invert
18.	**control**	command	plus	convey	convert
19.	**hold**	grow	grasp	ground	grit
20.	**agree**	actress	accept	account	accommodate

17. Smart or Stupid

Instruction: Write the matching synonyms from the Word Bank underneath the words in bold.

Word Bank

clever	ignorant	foolish	savvy	ludicrous
thick	perceptive	brainy	dumb	alert
sharp	bright	mindless	intelligent	genius
brainless	imbecile	brilliant	silly	dummy

Smart	**Stupid**

18. Yes or No Game

Instructions: Write "Yes" in Column B if the words in Column A are synonyms. If they are NOT synonyms, write "No" then write a synonym for the first word. Several synonyms are possible.

Column A	Column B
1. accelerate – quicken	
2. oblivious – aware	
3. hasten – dawdle	
4. pliable – rigid	
5. blatant – subtle	
6. tentative – definite	
7. hot – lukewarm	
8. metropolis – city	
9. up – alert	
10. cold – chilly	
11. baby – infant	
12. serene – town	
13. silent – quiet	
14. affection – fondness	
15. odor – mild	
16. master – slave	
17. liberty – freedom	
18. alliance – league	
19. decision – conflict	
20. guilty - innocent	

19. Odd One Out

Instruction: Find which word is the odd one out. Cross it out.

1.	affection	hate	love	like
2.	help	aid	belittle	assist
3.	forget	forgive	ignore	neglect
4.	enemy	challenger	antagonist	brother
5.	stay	allow	remain	wait
6.	virtue	decency	righteousness	immorality
7.	pull	push	pluck	yank
8.	decrease	descent	decline	desire
9.	absent	present	lacking	gone
10.	team	group	class	classroom
11.	joke	trick	prank	error
12.	stress	tension	prediction	pressure
13.	idea	liability	thought	concept
14.	one	two	letter	three
15.	golden	gilded	riches	ancient
16.	overtired	fatigued	weary	enthusiastic
17.	credence	skepticism	faith	trust
18.	promptness	tardiness	late	delay
19.	tools	equipment	attic	gear
20.	repetition	replication	recurrence	remorse

20. Big or Small

Instruction: Write the matching synonyms from the Word Bank underneath the words in bold.

Word Bank

substantial	petite	tiny	great	enormous
huge	slight	mighty	gigantic	colossal
diminutive	compact	insignificant	stupendous	massive
minuscule	microscopic	jumbo	baby	miniature

Big	**Small**

21. Antonyms

Instruction: Complete the antonym of the word in bold.

1. **important**   i r __ __ __ __ __ __ n t

2. **full**   e __ __ __ y

3. **disappointed**   s a __ __ __ __ __ e d

4. **forever**   t __ __ __ __ __ __ r y

5. **abundant**   s p __ __ __ e

6. **fake**   o r __ __ __ __ __ l

7. **serious**   t r __ __ __ __ l

8. **false**   t __ __ e

9. **supply**   d e __ __ __ d

10. **black**   w __ __ __ e

11. **reduce**   i n __ __ __ __ __ e

12. **occupied**   v a __ __ __ t

13. **cruel**   m e __ __ __ __ __ l

14. **leave**   s __ __ y

15. **for**   a g __ __ __ __ t

16. **pro**   c __ n

17. **abstract**   c o __ __ __ __ t e

18. **general**   s p __ __ __ __ __ c

19. **day**   n __ __ __ t

20. **freeze**   m __ __ t

22. Synonyms

Instruction: Find the synonym of the word in bold. Cross it out.

1.	**add**	remove	include	deduct	reduce
2.	**buy**	sell	sale	purchase	review
3.	**fear**	tired	fire	fright	belief
4.	**sit**	perch	stand	rise	device
5.	**late**	on time	delayed	beneath	below
6.	**inside**	outer	outside	inner	public
7.	**admit**	reflect	remember	try	confess
8.	**more**	less	fewer	additional	old
9.	**bring**	follow	quit	carry	leave
10.	**catch**	seize	dozen	correlate	respond
11.	**horror**	idea	terror	magnitude	drop
12.	**arrive**	come	leave	call	step
13.	**real**	ideal	imaginary	fake	actual
14.	**motion**	stand	sit	movement	word
15.	**avoid**	indulge	confront	ignore	oppose
16.	**love**	hate	heal	treat	adore
17.	**fail**	work	walk	flunk	sail
18.	**ready**	give	prepared	testing	trait
19.	**best**	pot	greatest	belittle	friend
20.	**similar**	alike	aloof	apart	different

23. Clean and Dirty

Instruction: Write the matching synonyms from the Word Bank underneath the words in bold.

Word Bank

unsoiled	filthy	washed	mucky	nasty
tidy	pure	spotless	scrubbed	greasy
unstained	contaminated	icky	sanitary	hygienic
stained	cleansed	foul	obscene	grimy

Clean	**Dirty**

24. Antonym

Instruction: Write the matching antonym from the Word Bank on the blank.

Word Bank

theory	asset	absence	belief	departure
take off	uphill	liquid	exit	safety
allegiance	proof	proximity	land	different
deport	import	anonymous	primary	inferior

1. **downhill** _____

2. **landing** _____

3. **fact** _____

4. **liability** _____

5. **admit** _____

6. **treason** _____

7. **entrance** _____

8. **sea** _____

9. **identical** _____

10. **presence** _____

11. **export** _____

12. **solid** _____

13. **danger** _____

14. **secondary** _____

15. **disbelief** _____

16. **superior** _____

17. **famous** _____

18. **arrival** _____

19. **guess** _____

20. **distance** _____

25. Synonyms

Instruction: Complete the synonym of the word in bold.

1. **share**   s p ___ ___ t

2. **simple**   p ___ ___ i n

3. **win**   t r ___ ___ ___ ___ h

4. **vacation**   h o ___ ___ ___ ___ y

5. **property**   b e ___ ___ ___ ___ ___ ___ g s

6. **anguish**   d i ___ ___ ___ ___ s s

7. **stop**   c e ___ ___ e

8. **cruelty**   b r ___ ___ ___ ___ ___ t y

9. **old**   e l ___ ___ ___ ___ y

10. **vote**   b a ___ ___ ___ t

11. **receive**   o b ___ ___ ___ n

12. **nation**   c ___ ___ ___ ___ r y

13. **study**   l e ___ ___ n

14. **contemporary**   c ___ ___ ___ ___ n t

15. **mission**   q u ___ ___ t

16. **young**   y o ___ ___ ___ ___ u l

17. **malicious**   m a ___ ___ ___ ___ ___ ___ n t

18. **tell**   i ___ ___ ___ ___ m

19. **film**   m ___ ___ ___ e

20. **wrong**   i n ___ ___ ___ ___ ___ ___ t

26. Similar and Different

Instruction: Write the matching synonyms from the Word Bank underneath the words in bold.

Word Bank

discrete	disparate	individual	comparable	equivalent
matching	dissimilar	akin	alike	incompatible
close	related	homogeneous	unusual	contrasting
analogous	resembling	distinct	inconsistent	diverse

Similar	**Different**

27. Antonyms

Instruction: Complete the antonym of the word in bold.

1. **wrong**   c o ___ ___ ___ ___ t

2. **dry**   h ___ ___ ___ d

3. **here**   t h ___ ___ e

4. **liquid**   s o ___ ___ d

5. **minimum**   m a ___ ___ ___ ___ m

6. **everybody**   n ___ ___ ___ ___ y

7. **tomorrow**   y e ___ ___ ___ ___ ___ ___ y

8. **present**   a b ___ ___ ___ t

9. **suburb**   c ___ ___ ___ e r

10. **exactly**   a p ___ ___ ___ ___ ___ ___ ___ ___ ___ y

11. **dead**   a ___ ___ ___ e

12. **exemplary**   o u ___ ___ ___ ___ ___ ___ u s

13. **unite**   d i ___ ___ ___ e

14. **hell**   h ___ ___ ___ ___ n

15. **top**   b ___ ___ ___ ___ m

16. **master**   s ___ ___ ___ ___ n t

17. **private**   p ___ ___ ___ ___ c

18. **foreigner**   n a ___ ___ ___ e

19. **best**   w ___ ___ ___ t

20. **teach**   l e ___ ___ n

28. Synonyms

Instruction: Find the synonym of the word in bold. Cross it out.

1.	**illness**	toothache	sickness	sailor	ship
2.	**monotony**	party	adventure	dullness	drowsy
3.	**peril**	jeopardy	safety	maps	diver
4.	**occasionally**	now	tomorrow	sometimes	later
5.	**reek**	perfume	aroma	stink	permit
6.	**tedious**	fun	boring	exciting	biting
7.	**vulnerable**	homeless	endangered	above	resilient
8.	**anguish**	pleasantry	surprise	suffice	suffering
9.	**wary**	attention	trustful	inattentive	cautious
10.	**keen**	allow	mean	keep	eager
11.	**woods**	trees	forest	mountain	field
12.	**revengeful**	lazy	salute	vindictive	tedious
13.	**panorama**	interior	scene	congestion	camera
14.	**supervise**	alarm	direct	follow	neglect
15.	**devotion**	convenient	deduct	reduce	loyalty
16.	**happiness**	flaw	boredom	joy	wonder
17.	**sleeplessness**	dreaming	insomnia	nightmare	apnea
18.	**show**	deteriorate	demonstrate	attend	devotion
19.	**eliminate**	colic	eradicate	convince	extreme
20.	**violently**	strict	forcefully	peacefully	rigorous

29. Fresh and Stale

Instruction: Write the matching synonyms from the Word Bank underneath the words in bold.

Word Bank

uncured	old	new	rotten	natural
spoiled	unspoiled	pristine	original	off
hardened	pure	unprocessed	rancid	unpreserved
decayed	dry	clean	musty	timeworn

Fresh	**Stale**

30. Odd One Out

Instruction: Find which word is the odd one out. Cross it out.

1.	closest	near	here	outside
2.	dirty	filthy	clean	stained
3.	message	data	information	book
4.	wish	desire	will	wound
5.	heal	injure	hurt	pain
6.	shine	sparkle	clean	musty
7.	destroy	demolish	derive	damage
8.	similar	equal	alike	apart
9.	relative	cousin	family	neighbor
10.	commence	finish	start	begin
11.	loyal	true	treacherous	faithful
12.	colorful	monochrome	animated	vivid
13.	spectrum	rainbow	iridescent	unicorn
14.	express	speedy	superb	fast
15.	dusk	sunrise	evening	night
16.	inside	inaugurate	inner	indoors
17.	prudent	youthful	young	juvenile
18.	proud	limit	restrict	ban
19.	watch	observe	see	outburst
20.	wreck	repair	mend	restore

31. Yes or No Game

Instructions: Write "Yes" in Column B if the words in Column A are synonyms. If they are NOT synonyms, write "No" then write a synonym for the first word. Several synonyms are possible.

Column A	Column B
1. scare – frighten	
2. bald – bold	
3. silly – foolish	
4. stinky – aroma	
5. run – stop	
6. nice – delightful	
7. rare – uncommon	
8. inside – within	
9. without – whether	
10. rapid – fast	
11. pal – foe	
12. near – distant	
13. wise – wide	
14. wild – tame	
15. insipid – interesting	
16. automatic – car	
17. elephantine – mammoth	
18. illusionist – magician	
19. applaud - clap	
20. audience - spectators	

32. Try and Quit

Instruction: Write the matching synonyms from the Word Bank underneath the words in bold.

Word Bank

test	retire	withdraw	attempt	leave
seek	abandon	strive	aspire	cease
drop	effort	taste	endeavor	check
left	experiment	desert	discontinue	resign

Try	**Quit**

33. Synonyms

Instruction: Complete the synonym of the word in bold.

1. **kind**   n ___ ___ e

2. **complex**   c o ___ ___ ___ ___ ___ ___ ___ e d

3. **glad**   p l ___ ___ ___ e d

4. **noisy**   l ___ ___ d

5. **tiny**   p e ___ ___ t e

6. **lady**   w ___ ___ ___ n

7. **sad**   u n ___ ___ ___ ___ y

8. **huge**   e n ___ ___ ___ ___ ___ s

9. **interesting**   f a ___ ___ ___ ___ ___ ___ ___ n g

10. **strange**   u n ___ ___ ___ ___ l

11. **loose**   b a ___ ___ y

12. **very hot**   s c ___ ___ ___ ___ ___ ___ g

13. **squander**   w ___ ___ t e

14. **ridiculous**   a b ___ ___ ___ d

15. **gigantic**   h ___ ___ e

16. **cautious**   c a ___ ___ ___ ___ l

17. **differ**   d i ___ ___ ___ ___ e e

18. **fearless**   b ___ ___ v e

19. **achieve**   s u ___ ___ ___ ___ d

20. **irritate**   a n ___ ___ y

34. Antonyms

Instruction: Find the antonym of the word in bold. Cross it out.

1.	**live**	lie	die	deny	cry
2.	**complete**	entire	partial	fraud	depart
3.	**summer**	day	spring	winter	autumn
4.	**dirty**	heavy	clan	true	clean
5.	**first**	second	last	minute	later
6.	**sob**	cry	laugh	accept	cold
7.	**destroy**	cover	peace	build	war
8.	**sick**	hard	ill	healthy	poor
9.	**rare**	common	contrast	command	convoy
10.	**reliable**	isolate	trusting	friend	untrustworthy
11.	**mend**	qualify	destroy	center	bend
12.	**firm**	bleed	bond	tough	soft
13.	**odd**	unusual	peculiar	normal	strange
14.	**injustice**	fairness	fight	wrong	freedom
15.	**war**	cry	fight	soldier	peace
16.	**fat**	obese	skinny	grand	great
17.	**man**	boy	masculine	woman	guy
18.	**old**	pension	retired	youthful	scar
19.	**far**	close	there	behind	below
20.	**city**	country	town	center	market

35. Problem or Solution

Instruction: Write the matching synonyms from the Word Bank underneath the words in bold.

Word Bank

trouble	result	issue	answer	challenge
determination	difficulty	finding	solving	key
complication	explication	worry	nuisance	obstacle
predicament	conclusion	concern	resolution	explanation

Problem	**Solution**

36. Odd One Out

Instruction: Find which word is the odd one out. Cross it out.

1.	dear	kind	nice	nasty
2.	mindful	brilliant	thankful	smart
3.	irritate	agitate	accurate	annoy
4.	sell	buy	purchase	acquire
5.	deal	break	contract	agreement
6.	among	apart	separately	independently
7.	steel	pierce	slit	cut
8.	pair	couple	match	dice
9.	live	recede	dwell	reside
10.	remote	aloof	distant	friendly
11.	fiction	information	data	facts
12.	end	abort	commence	terminate
13.	error	missile	mistake	misconception
14.	launch	introduce	instigate	shift
15.	mellow	amicable	deluxe	warm
16.	era	condition	period	epoch
17.	situation	style	circumstances	state
18.	mushroom	bacteria	germs	bacilli
19.	heal	rehabilitate	heat	remedy
20.	blow	whistle	toot	shiver

37. Synonyms

Instruction: Complete the synonym of the word in bold.

1. **remote**   d ___ ___ ___ ___ n t

2. **kin**   r e ___ ___ ___ ___ ___ e

3. **gracious**   p l ___ ___ ___ ___ ___ t

4. **impersonator**   i ___ ___ ___ ___ ___ e r

5. **drag**   p ___ ___ l

6. **wary**   c ___ ___ ___ ___ ___ u s

7. **loot**   s p ___ ___ l s

8. **propose**   s u ___ ___ ___ s t

9. **prolong**   e x ___ ___ ___ d

10. **modest**   h ___ ___ ___ ___ e

11. **fearless**   b ___ ___ ___ e

12. **beneficial**   h e ___ ___ ___ u l

13. **resolve**   s e ___ ___ l e

14. **dupe**   d e ___ ___ ___ ___ e

15. **reside**   d ___ ___ ___ l

16. **gathering**   m e ___ ___ ___ n g

17. **bespoke**   t a ___ ___ ___ ___ e d

18. **aloof**   d i ___ ___ ___ ___ t

19 **negligent**   c a ___ ___ ___ ___ ___ s

20. **fire**   b l ___ ___ e

38. Luck or Misfortune

Instruction: Write the matching synonyms from the Word Bank underneath the words in bold.

Word Bank

fortune	calamity	chance	mishap	fate
destiny	misery	catastrophe	serendipity	fluke
tribulation	disaster	fortuity	difficulty	providence
windfall	hardship	tragedy	setback	happenstance

Luck	**Misfortune**

39. Antonyms

Instruction: Find the antonym of the word in bold. Cross it out.

1.	**maintain**	murder	stab	kill	neglect
2.	**ascend**	leap	grow	mount	sink
3.	**revulsion**	delight	violence	disgust	avenge
4.	**servant**	master	slavish	laborer	attendant
5.	**distinctive**	common	divide	deny	different
6.	**angry**	troubled	irritable	difficult	calm
7.	**grit**	bold	cowardice	grease	level
8.	**callous**	hot-tempered	immature	hollow	compassionate
9.	**astute**	quick-witted	clever	charming	stupid
10.	**combat**	fight	conflict	quarrel	peace
11.	**innocent**	steal	guilty	fault	major
12.	**subtle**	carefree	artistic	obvious	nice
13.	**modest**	humble	straight	boastful	shy
14.	**dull**	trying	interesting	malevolent	boredom
15.	**shrink**	tall	playful	expand	extent
16.	**bitter**	coarse	quiet	sweet	enigma
17.	**glow**	fire	flare	darkness	light
18.	**reward**	praise	award	punish	plain
19.	**final**	initial	mandatory	clever	exit
20.	**agree**	rebound	recover	reduce	reject

40. Synonym

Instruction: Write the matching synonym from the Word Bank on the blank.

Word Bank

kind	follow	emit	hide	gather
fake	mercy	result	fair	dissipate
agitate	adversity	weak	attentive	brute
shortage	talk	display	brief	impure

1. **frail** _____
2. **disguise** _____
3. **accumulate** _____
4. **calamity** _____
5. **savage** _____
6. **alert** _____
7. **disperse** _____
8. **humane** _____
9. **disturb** _____
10. **pursue** _____
11. **consequence** _____
12. **spurious** _____
13. **deficiency** _____
14. **speak** _____
15. **discharge** _____
16. **polluted** _____
17. **short** _____
18. **compassion** _____
19. **exhibit** _____
20. **equitable** _____

41. Loud and Quiet

Instruction: Write the matching synonyms from the Word Bank underneath the words in bold.

Word Bank

peace	noisy	deafening	boisterous	tranquil
roaring	rowdy	placid	blaring	clamorous
subdued	silent	thunderous	pacify	resounding
still	hush	serene	soundless	ear-splitting

Loud	**Quiet**

42. Yes or No Game

Instructions: Write "Yes" in Column B if the words in Column A are antonyms. If they are NOT antonyms, write "No" then write an antonym for the first word. Several antonyms are possible.

Column A	Column B
1. strive – attempt	
2. peculiar – ordinary	
3. large – miniature	
4. remain – go	
5. hurriedly – quietly	
6. allow – prevent	
7. cover – expose	
8. humane – home	
9. comfort – distress	
10. curious – cured	
11. assemble – scatter	
12. delighted – cheerful	
13. enmity – hatred	
14. blossom – decay	
15. guest – host	
16. reveal – conceal	
17. ascend – fall	
18. boastful – modest	
19. discontinue – deny	
20. forceful – wimpy	

43. Odd One Out

Instruction: Find which word is the odd one out. Cross it out.

1. useless   vain   futile   conflict
2. invader   guest   assailant   attacker
3. lower   inferior   upper   subordinate
4. friendship   apathy   indifference   unconcern
5. bold   brave   darling   daring
6. doubt   distrust   disbelief   disregard
7. uneven   rough   irregular   smooth
8. misunderstand   misinterpret   misapprehend   misuse
9. receive   collect   hoard   gather
10. firm   hard   ribbon   rigid
11. joy   delight   plea   pleasure
12. confine   detain   announce   imprison
13. unity   division   disunity   conflict
14. harmful   great   defective   spoiled
15. awake   asleep   drowsy   dreaming
16. road   street   boulevard   traffic
17. prosperity   riches   poverty   success
18. victory   win   accomplish   defeat
19. petite   gross   slim   tiny
20. gradual   hurried   quick   prompt

44. Synonyms

Instruction: Complete the synonym of the word in bold.

1.	**riches**	w ___ ___ ___ t h
2.	**power**	f o ___ ___ e
3.	**music**	m e ___ ___ ___ y
4.	**look**	w ___ ___ c h
5.	**assist**	h ___ ___ p
6.	**hop**	j ___ ___ p
7.	**award**	p r ___ ___ e
8.	**brilliant**	d a ___ ___ ___ ___ n g
9.	**cautious**	c a ___ ___ ___ ___ l
10.	**celebration**	p ___ ___ ___ y
11.	**affect**	t o ___ ___ h
12.	**end**	f ___ ___ ___ s h
13.	**money**	c ___ ___ h
14.	**glossy**	s h ___ ___ y
15.	**sad**	g l ___ ___ m y
16.	**confined**	c r ___ ___ ___ e d
17.	**crisp**	c r ___ ___ ___ ___ y
18.	**amazement**	w ___ ___ ___ e r
19.	**wash**	b ___ ___ h e
20.	**victory**	s ___ ___ ___ ___ s s

45. Guilty or Innocent

Instruction: Write the matching synonyms from the Word Bank underneath the words in bold.

Word Bank

ashamed	responsible	untainted	pure	culpable
naive	contrite	remorseful	blameless	sinful
blamable	repentant	chaste	inoffensive	convicted
vindicated	acquitted	criminal	faultless	exonerated

Guilty	**Innocent**

46. Antonyms

Instruction: Find the antonym of the word in bold. Cross it out.

1.	**father**	daddy	papa	mother	priest
2.	**intuition**	clairvoyance	instinct	divination	intellect
3.	**miss**	skip	forget	hit	pay
4.	**sister**	nurse	nun	chum	brother
5.	**modern**	modest	older	contemporary	early
6.	**several**	few	away	timid	many
7.	**ask**	answer	data	correct	information
8.	**long**	large	giant	short	shallow
9.	**husband**	adult	woman	man	wife
10.	**desperate**	serious	depressed	hopeful	hopeless
11.	**order**	law	force	chaos	line
12.	**awake**	wide	dire	asleep	ahead
13.	**heat**	hot	summer	winter	cold
14.	**keep**	give up	retain	hold on to	remain
15.	**constant**	equal	changeable	alike	stall
16.	**later**	delay	deny	earlier	faster
17.	**angel**	devil	pretty	church	sin
18.	**children**	kids	adults	infants	babies
19.	**affirmative**	close	negative	forward	hopeful
20.	**all**	few	none	million	less

47. Synonym

Instruction: Write the matching synonym from the Word Bank on the blank.

Word Bank

view	marvel	terrible	emergency	manage
hit	return	evening	cook	nothing
sweet	stimulating	destroy	belittle	known
wet	genuine	kind	exaggerate	train

1. **crisis** _____
2. **popular** _____
3. **sight** _____
4. **real** _____
5. **hospitable** _____
6. **exciting** _____
7. **sugary** _____
8. **discipline** _____
9. **control** _____
10. **ghastly** _____
11. **bake** _____
12. **overstate** _____
13. **miracle** _____
14. **demolish** _____
15. **smack** _____
16. **moist** _____
17. **revisit** _____
18. **disparage** _____
19. **dusk** _____
20. **nil** _____

48. Odd One Out

Instruction: Find which word is the odd one out. Cross it out.

1.	foreign	alien	stranger	host
2.	evaluate	detailed	appraise	consider
3.	territory	district	finite	region
4.	reflection	mistake	failure	error
5.	punctual	right	incomparable	exact
6.	complex	intricate	wicked	complicated
7.	compound	indicate	show	imply
8.	fright	battle	combat	fight
9.	fracture	break	crack	squeak
10.	create	diminutive	produce	generate
11.	area	zone	lot	neutral
12.	honor	respect	default	appreciate
13.	rigid	soft	gentle	smooth
14.	stretch	shorten	compress	compact
15.	isolated	determined	faraway	distant
16.	mundane	likely	possible	probable
17.	hail	applaud	appraise	advertize
18.	fake	fragile	fraud	phony
19.	unnatural	abnormal	irregular	irrelevant
20.	impediment	spread	broadcast	distribute

49. Antonyms

Instruction: Find the antonym of the word in bold. Cross it out.

1. **hard**	melting	soft	dry	powder
2. **lose**	invent	find	misplace	deny
3. **under**	behind	above	below	last
4. **cold**	delicious	freezing	warm	wet
5. **short**	sharp	small	tall	little
6. **messy**	curious	organized	tired	bored
7. **dark**	down	sun	light	deep
8. **late**	early	behind	tight	correct
9. **empty**	soft	hard	full	dry
10. **close**	try	near	adjacent	far
11. **wet**	silly	moist	spray	dry
12. **small**	entire	enormous	adequate	portable
13. **near**	nearby	at hand	far	approach
14. **heavy**	rude	hefty	thick	light
15. **wide**	spacious	large	vast	narrow
16. **far**	near	distant	remote	away
17. **fast**	lively	slow	swift	rapidly
18. **hungry**	full	starving	hollow	thirsty
19. **intelligent**	clever	brilliant	dumb	sharp
20. **exit**	entrance	end	withdrawal	depart

50. Friend or Foe

Instruction: Write the matching synonyms from the Word Bank underneath the words in bold.

Word Bank

enemy	opponent	buddy	companion	rival
ally	comrade	mate	attacker	pal
associate	competitor	fellow	partner	antagonist
supporter	adversary	challenger	arch-enemy	disputant

Friend	Foe

51. Yes or No Game

Instructions: Write "Yes" beside the word in bold if they are antonyms. If they are NOT antonyms, write "No" then write an antonym for the first word. Several antonyms are possible.

Column 1	Column 2
Column 1	**Column 2**

Column 1

1. **attentive – ahead**

2. **slim – fat**

3. **thin – narrow**

4. **sick – healthy**

5. **banish – invite**

6. **bluff – truth**

7. **attack – strike**

8. **diminish – extend**

9. **emerge – disappear**

10. **furtive – secret**

11. **luminous – shiny**

12. **multitude – hundreds**

13. **persistent – stubborn**

14. **pristine – pure**

15. **replenish – empty**

16. **scarce – lots**

17. **scurry – amble**

18. **sociable – introverted**

19. **unsightly – pleasant**

20. **vigilant – disinterested**

52. Antonyms

Instruction: Complete the antonym of the word in bold.

1. **affirm**   d ___ ___ y
2. **recent**   p ___ ___ t
3. **ancient**   c o ___ ___ ___ ___ ___ ___ ___ ___ r y
4. **vice**   v i ___ ___ u e
5. **voluntary**   o b ___ ___ ___ ___ ___ ___ r y
6. **compulsory**   o p ___ ___ ___ ___ a l
7. **consent**   d i ___ ___ ___ n t
8. **indifferent**   c a ___ ___ ___ g
9. **elated**   m i ___ ___ ___ ___ ___ l e
10. **cheerful**   d o ___ ___ ___ ___ s t
11. **lament**   c e ___ ___ ___ ___ ___ ___ e
12. **myriad**   f ___ w
13. **stupid**   c l ___ ___ ___ r
14. **animosity**   g o ___ ___ ___ ___ ___ l l
15. **ambiguous**   o b ___ ___ ___ u s
16. **negate**   c ___ ___ ___ ___ ___ r m
17. **prompt**   s ___ ___ w
18. **hostile**   f ___ ___ ___ ___ ___ ___ l y
19. **correct**   f ___ ___ ___ e
20. **vague**   p r ___ ___ ___ s e

53. Odd One Out

Instruction: Find which word is the odd one out. Cross it out.

1.	argument	disagreement	dispute	contract
2.	control	conflict	manage	supervise
3.	interrogate	investigate	question	answer
4.	teach	learn	find out	discover
5.	write	right	inscribe	note
6.	sight	see	sea	look
7.	dessert	abandon	desert	forsake
8.	allow	permit	let	leave
9.	forget	suffer	pain	discomfort
10.	entertain	amuse	amulet	please
11.	quest	mission	task	question
12.	interact	petrified	socialize	communicate
13.	dishonest	disbeliever	sceptic	unbeliever
14.	typical	usual	regular	abnormal
15.	scarce	copious	luxuriant	rampant
16.	infamous	honorable	commendable	meritorious
17.	despicable	contemptible	ignominious	philanthropy
18.	censure	reprimand	reproach	culpability
19.	affiliation	coalition	confederation	commemoration
20.	allure	entice	aside	attract

54. Synonym

Instruction: Write the matching synonym from the Word Bank on the blank.

Word Bank

answer	retort	clumsy	ask	assault
petrified	unconventional	unbeliever	abominable	loyal
defame	slander	bountiful	detest	plaudit
allegation	acquit	munificence	laudable	tear

1. **awkward** _____
2. **besmirch** _____
3. **terrified** _____
4. **assail** _____
5. **ovation** _____
6. **abundant** _____
7. **reply** _____
8. **accusation** _____
9. **abhor** _____
10. **faithful** _____
11. **loathsome** _____
12. **exonerate** _____
13. **atheist** _____
14. **commendable** _____
15. **rejoinder** _____
16. **largesse** _____
17. **laceration** _____
18. **inquire** _____
19. **defame** _____
20. **eccentric** _____

55. Hide and Seek

Instruction: Write the matching synonyms from the Word Bank underneath the words in bold.

Word Bank

conceal	look for	cover	mask	scout
shield	quest	shroud	hunt	camouflage
envelop	pursue	secret	desire	bury
disguise	search	browse	root out	forage

Hide	**Seek**

56. Odd One Out

Instruction: Find which word is the odd one out. Cross it out.

1. humble   modest   arrogant   submissive
2. blasphemy   curse   swear   bless
3. trivial   serious   unimportant   minor
4. gather   disperse   scatter   spread
5. foreigner   stranger   immigrant   native
6. strong   feeble   fearless   brave
7. enlarge   elongate   expand   shrink
8. guilty   innocent   culpable   convicted
9. repair   destroy   demolish   dismantle
10. forgiving   vengeful   vindictive   angry
11. disgusting   abominable   loathsome   lurch
12. calumny   libel   slander   abundant
13. disarray   messiness   dispatcher   disorderliness
14. loiter   dawdle   stall   hasten
15. diminutive   miniature   monumental   miniscule
16. insignificant   eminent   esteemed   famous
17. crazy   indolent   languid   lazy
18. abundant   scarce   bountiful   plenty
19. negligent   careless   careful   irresponsible
20. evaluate   appraise   assess   associate

57. Yes or No Game

Instructions: Write "Yes" in Column B if the words in Column A are antonyms. If they are NOT antonyms, write "No" then write an antonym for the first word. Several antonyms are possible.

Column A	Column B
1. disturbed – peaceful	
2. belligerent – bellicose	
3. fractious – calm	
4. militant – militia	
5. consensus – agreement	
6. harmony – incompatibility	
7. unanimity – difference	
8. truce – peace	
9. agree – concur	
10. ameliorate – worsen	
11. subdue – put down	
12. relief – burden	
13. appease – provoke	
14. resolve – absolve	
15. yearn – covet	
16. adversity – difficulty	
17. transparent – opaque	
18. virtue – vice	
19. defeat – victory	
20. folly – wisdom	

58. High and Low

Instruction: Write the matching synonyms from the Word Bank underneath the words in bold.

Word Bank

towering	despicable	elevated	miserable	inferior
abject	tall	blue	soaring	upper
gloomy	down	above	base	lifted
escalated	heightened	lofty	downcast	sunken

High	**Low**

59. Synonym

Instruction: Write the matching synonym from the Word Bank on the blank.

Word Bank

placate	palliate	addition	lure	wheedle
affable	disagreeable	vicious	incognito	affinity
appropriate	resist	antiquated	animosity	excuse
antipathy	repel	languid	imbue	outmoded

1. **passé** _____

2. **mollify** _____

3. **amicable** _____

4. **savage** _____

5. **alleviate** _____

6. **animus** _____

7. **apt** _____

8. **extension** _____

9. **antagonism** _____

10. **entice** _____

11. **rapport** _____

12. **extenuate** _____

13. **ancient** _____

14. **unpleasant** _____

15. **coax** _____

16. **anonymous** _____

17. **repulse** _____

18. **listless** _____

19. **permeate** _____

20. **oppose** _____

60. Antonyms

Instruction: Complete the antonym of the word in bold.

1. **respect**   d i __ __ __ __ __ __ c t

2. **restore**   b r __ __ k

3. **lengthen**   a b __ __ __ __ __ __ t e

4. **commence**   c o __ __ __ __ d e

5. **satisfy**   f r __ __ __ __ __ t e

6. **damage**   r e __ __ __ r

7. **restrained**   u n r __ __ __ __ __ __ n e d

8. **subtle**   c r __ __ e

9. **terminate**   b __ __ __ n

10. **fatigue**   e n __ __ __ y

11. **diminish**   i n __ __ __ __ s e

12. **overlook**   n o __ __ __ e

13. **reckless**   c a __ __ __ __ u s

14. **kind-hearted**   h e __ __ __ __ __ s s

15. **lose**   a c __ __ __ r e

16. **meek**   b __ __ d

17. **attentive**   i n __ __ __ __ __ __ __ v e

18. **thrive**   l a __ __ __ __ s h

19. **enhance**   d i __ __ __ __ s h

20. **calm**   t e __ __ __ __ __ __ __ __ __ a l

61. Intense and Shallow

Instruction: Write the matching synonyms from the Word Bank underneath the words in bold.

Word Bank

profound	surface	superficial	ardent	foolish
unimportant	strong	rich	trivial	resonant
petty	frivolous	glib	serious	silly
extensive	flimsy	immeasurable	earnest	great

Intense	**Shallow**

62. Yes or No Game

Instructions: Write "Yes" in Column B if the words in Column A are antonyms. If they are NOT antonyms, write "No" then write an antonym for the first word. Several antonyms are possible.

Column A	Column B
1. apathy – enthusiasm	
2. lassitude – energetic	
3. active – lethargic	
4. flawless – blemished	
5. shy – unabashed	
6. heartlessness – indefinite	
7. aroma – stink	
8. profuse – sparse	
9. gloomy – dark	
10. hostile – violent	
11. mischievous – malevolent	
12. benevolent – unkind	
13. aerate – deflate	
14. decrease – decease	
15. solemn – light hearted	
16. egoistic – boastful	
17. germane – appropriate	
18. inimical – helpful	
19. perfunctory – thorough	
20. despondent – despair	

63. Synonym

Instruction: Write the matching synonym from the Word Bank on the blank.

Word Bank

remorseful	apex	apropos	crude	authentic
apprentice	eloquent	tyrannical	capricious	determined
grueling	squabble	augur	poise	parsimonious
hackneyed	amazing	banish	elated	elongate

1. **summit** _____
2. **fickle** _____
3. **ecstatic** _____
4. **rudimentary** _____
5. **apt** _____
6. **arduous** _____
7. **contrite** _____
8. **bicker** _____
9. **prolong** _____
10. **articulate** _____
11. **bode** _____
12. **genuine** _____
13. **stingy** _____
14. **aplomb** _____
15. **novice** _____
16. **resolute** _____
17. **banal** _____
18. **autocratic** _____
19. **exile** _____
20. **remarkable** _____

64. Odd One Out

Instruction: Find which word is the odd one out. Cross it out.

1. amateur   professional   expert   knowledgeable
2. blunt   sharp   dull   rounded
3. calm   agitated   frustrated   angry
4. hopeless   despair   hope   desperate
5. doubt   attest   suspicion   hesitation
6. demand   ask   supply   request
7. agree   annoy   disturb   agitate
8. soothe   peaceful   calm   reproduce
9. fresh   recent   new   stale
10. grin   frown   smile   laugh
11. nasty   hasty   offensive   malicious
12. hazard   peril   disorder   danger
13. fail   succeed   achieve   accomplish
14. jump   leap   bounce   crawl
15. fraction   fraternity   fragment   snippet
16. favorite   dear   favored   flavored
17. blemished   flawless   intact   sound
18. prefer   choose   select   chomp
19. disagree   veto   prohibit   forbid
20. restriction   reduction   reproduction   cutback

65. Synonyms

Instruction: Complete the synonym of the word in bold.

1. **wrath**   a ___ ___ ___ r

2. **unnatural**   p r ___ ___ ___ ___ ___ ___ ___ u s

3. **calamity**   d i ___ ___ ___ ___ ___ r

4. **flinch**   w ___ ___ ___ e

5. **superficial**   s h ___ ___ ___ ___ w

6. **stripe**   s t ___ ___ a k

7. **glitter**   s p ___ ___ ___ ___ l e

8. **rectify**   c o ___ ___ ___ c t

9. **affect**   i n ___ ___ ___ ___ ___ c e

10. **halt**   t e ___ ___ ___ ___ ___ t e

11. **perseverance**   t e ___ ___ ___ ___ t y

12. **baffle**   p e ___ ___ ___ ___ e x

13. **superfluous**   u n ___ ___ ___ ___ ___ ___ ___ r y

14. **treacherous**   d e ___ ___ ___ ___ ___ u l

15. **endeavor**   v e ___ ___ ___ r e

16. **offensive**   i m ___ ___ ___ ___ n t

17. **supernatural**   o c ___ ___ ___ t

18. **monotonous**   t e ___ ___ ___ u s

19. **well-being**   w e ___ ___ ___ r e

20. **useless**   f ___ ___ ___ l e

66. Dark and Light

Instruction: Write the matching synonyms from the Word Bank underneath the words in bold.

Word Bank

gloomy	illumination	black	pale	night
brightness	obscure	shine	radiant	bright
grim	dismal	shady	glow	dreary
dim	nightfall	clear	fair	lamp

Dark	**Light**

67. Antonym

Instruction: Write the matching antonym from the Word Bank on the blank.

Word Bank

purify	agreeable	restriction	delay	benevolence
accept	cruelty	assert	tractable	misunderstand
superior	indifferent	constructive	conquer	tardy
retain	love	eradicate	fake	strong

1. **speed up** _____
2. **abolish** _____
3. **deny** _____
4. **obstinate** _____
5. **disagreeable** _____
6. **destructive** _____
7. **hate** _____
8. **reject** _____
9. **propagate** _____
10. **understand** _____
11. **surrender** _____
12. **authentic** _____
13. **mercy** _____
14. **malice** _____
15. **inferior** _____
16. **taint** _____
17. **interested** _____
18. **freedom** _____
19. **punctual** _____
20. **frail** _____

68. Odd One Out

Instruction: Find which word is the odd one out. Cross it out.

1.	sleepy	tired	chewy	drowsy
2.	tiny	little	minor	furry
3.	rock	music	pebble	stone
4.	write	right	correct	exact
5.	same	lame	equal	alike
6.	noisy	loud	curious	rowdy
7.	auspicious	inauspicious	promising	fortunate
8.	aim	goal	target	adjective
9.	chant	opportunity	possibility	chance
10.	sanguinity	pessimism	optimism	hope
11.	reflect	reverberate	mirror	center
12.	recreate	retire	create	reinvent
13.	resolution	decision	determination	hesitation
14.	figurative	solve	resolve	figure
15.	guide	bachelor	usher	escort
16.	determination	self-command	insane	willpower
17.	consume	ingest	intestine	eat
18.	desire	craving	addiction	adhesion
19.	consume	devour	down	fully
20.	bloated	starved	ravenous	famished

69. Yes or No Game

Instructions: Write "Yes" in Column B if the words in Column A are antonyms. If they are NOT antonyms, write "No" then write an antonym for the first word. Several antonyms are possible.

Column A	Column B
1. fussy – proper	
2. shallow – deep	
3. untruthful – honest	
4. bleak – cheerful	
5. veneration – disrespect	
6. bestow – beneath	
7. remorse – regret	
8. rustic – rural	
9. pernicious – safe	
10. frail – healthy	
11. flair – inability	
12. hazy – clear	
13. precise – exact	
14. serenity – anxiety	
15. lustrous – dim	
16. jocular – serious	
17. melancholic – sadness	
18. lavish – generous	
19. mellifluous – melodious	
20. bemoan – regret	

70. Synonym

Instruction: Write the matching synonym from the Word Bank on the blank.

Word Bank

benevolent	deteriorate	confiscate	adulation	gloomy
toxic	limited	scorn	mischievous	immaculate
ameliorate	unpleasant	invulnerable	awe	great
paradox	grow	filthy	principal	decrease

1. **seize** _____

2. **admiration** _____

3. **poisonous** _____

4. **disrespect** _____

5. **charitable** _____

6. **naughty** _____

7. **improve** _____

8. **worsen** _____

9. **restricted** _____

10. **decline** _____

11. **somber** _____

12. **colossal** _____

13. **develop** _____

14. **wonder** _____

15. **pristine** _____

16. **obnoxious** _____

17. **chief** _____

18. **contradiction** _____

19. **invincible** _____

20. **dirty** _____

71. Open or Close

Instruction: Write the matching synonyms from the Word Bank underneath the words in bold.

Word Bank

candid	clear	suspend	honest	finalize
finish	free	unlock	start	end
begin	initiate	commence	terminate	complete
conclude	direct	shut	stop	cease

Open	Close

72. Odd One Out

Instruction: Find which word is the odd one out. Cross it out.

1.	agony	anguish	comfort	pain
2.	success	security	safety	sanctuary
3.	myriad	scarcity	plenty	a lot
4.	gratify	pleasure	satisfy	disappoint
5.	puncture	hole	drill	punctual
6.	fatigued	obsolete	tired	weary
7.	ignite	excite	thrill	exhilarate
8.	cultivate	labor	work	toil
9.	accumulate	accentuate	gather	collect
10.	deliver	expel	donate	receive
11.	add	deduct	total	count
12.	understand	comprehend	grasp	gradual
13.	ameliorate	improve	antiquated	upgrade
14.	instinctive	automatic	manual	reflexive
15.	standard	normal	average	unique
16.	consequential	diverse	significant	important
17.	senseless	illogical	irrational	purposeful
18.	present	tomorrow	later	afterward
19.	unswerving	consistent	steady	irregular
20.	justify	explain	refute	rationalize

73. Yes or No Game

Instructions: Write "Yes" in Column B if the words in Column A are antonyms. If they are NOT antonyms, write "No" then write an antonym for the first word. Several antonyms are possible.

Column A	Column B
1. defeat – triumph	
2. folly – foolish	
3. collect – acquire	
4. imprudent – wise	
5. peace – war	
6. miser – spendthrift	
7. magnify – diminish	
8. vacate – occupy	
9. discharge – deteriorate	
10. acclaim – prestige	
11. obscurity – villainy	
12. famous – popular	
13. intensify – amplify	
14. allay – lessen	
15. splurge – save	
16. expend – store	
17. porous – impervious	
18. forgo – keep	
19. wan – flushed	
20. dense – compact	

74. Vacant and Occupied

Instruction: Write the matching synonyms from the Word Bank underneath the words in bold.

Word Bank

empty	blank	engaged	void	free
deserted	preoccupied	vacuous	employed	uninhabited
taken	available	full	abandoned	devoid
working	inhabited	active	involved	busy

Vacant	Occupied

75. Synonym

Instruction: Write the matching synonym from the Word Bank on the blank.

Word Bank

alluring	deception	demolition	garnish	faithfulness
secret	honored	anguish	aversion	direct
lively	sympathy	conversant	friendly	skillful
destitute	instructive	unconventional	construct	gaiety

1. **deceit** _____
2. **compassion** _____
3. **decorate** _____
4. **animated** _____
5. **talented** _____
6. **enticing** _____
7. **informed** _____
8. **distress** _____
9. **poor** _____
10. **destruction** _____
11. **forge** _____
12. **candid** _____
13. **confidential** _____
14. **eccentric** _____
15. **dislike** _____
16. **joy** _____
17. **fidelity** _____
18. **cordial** _____
19. **respected** _____
20. **didactic** _____

76. Odd One Out

Instruction: Find which word is the odd one out. Cross it out.

1.	grief	anguish	guilt	sadness
2.	imperious	superior	arrogant	triumph
3.	inanimate	inert	lively	non-living
4.	laughter	lament	cry	sorrow
5.	hatred	melancholy	gloomy	depressed
6.	pensive	thoughtful	contemplative	reckless
7.	renown	honored	misdeed	acclaimed
8.	wild	domesticated	tame	docile
9.	reprove	reprimand	scold	satisfy
10.	impeach	disgrace	shame	ignominy
11.	pleasant	fulsome	insincere	fawning
12.	pillage	loot	plunder	valuable
13.	rumor	vilify	rail	revile
14.	haste	dawdle	drag	follow
15.	atone	expiate	explain	make amends
16.	reimburse	sell	repay	refund
17.	boorish	ill-mannered	neanderthal	refined
18.	forbid	formidable	impressive	terrific
19.	restless	fidgety	jittery	relaxed
20.	blunt	bland	flat	vapid

77. New Year, Old Socks

Instruction: Write the matching synonyms from the Word Bank underneath the words in bold.

Word Bank

original	current	former	contemporary	mature
novel	unprecedented	bygone	fresh	aged
worn	avant-garde	medieval	unknown	remote
modern	shabby	antique	archaic	past

New Year	**Old Socks**

78. Yes or No Game

Instructions: Write "Yes" in Column B if the words in Column A are antonyms. If they are NOT antonyms, write "No" then write an antonym for the first word. Several antonyms are possible.

Column A	Column B
Column A	**Column B**
1. entire – partial	
2. brief – short	
3. broad – wide	
4. wicked – evil	
5. strange – creative	
6. harsh – pleasant	
7. restive – restless	
8. chide – praise	
9. deny – negate	
10. avert – prevent	
11. mutilate – mend	
12. luminous – gloomy	
13. interesting – riveting	
14. barren – fertile	
15. irritate – bother	
16. bewitch – repel	
17. inane – ingenious	
18. verify – invalidate	
19. approximate – estimate	
20. appreciate – recognize	

79. Synonyms

Instruction: Complete the synonym of the word in bold.

1. **considerable**   s u ___ ___ ___ ___ ___ ___ ___ a l

2. **demand**   r e ___ ___ ___ ___ t

3. **chuckle**   g i ___ ___ l e

4. **walk**   s t ___ ___ l l

5. **glance**   g l ___ ___ ___ ___ e

6. **love**   a f ___ ___ ___ ___ ___ ___ n

7. **mournful**   s o ___ ___ ___ ___ ___ u l

8. **attractive**   p l ___ ___ ___ ___ n g

9. **purified**   r e ___ ___ ___ e d

10. **marvelous**   e x ___ ___ ___ ___ ___ ___ ___ ___ ___ r y

11. **tiny**   t e ___ ___ y

12. **compact**   p ___ ___ ___ e d

13. **kind**   c o ___ ___ ___ ___ ___ ___ ___ t e

14. **jocular**   f ___ ___ ___ y

15. **amusing**   h u ___ ___ ___ ___ ___ s

16. **funny**   w i ___ ___ y

17. **jovial**   j ___ ___ ___ ___ d

18. **stroll**   a m ___ ___ e

19. **astonishing**   s t u ___ ___ ___ ___ g

20. **respect**   a d ___ ___ ___ ___ ___ ___ o n

80. Antonym

Instruction: Write the matching antonym from the Word Bank on the blank.

Word Bank

carelessness	simplicity	disturbed	antipathy	discouraged
dawdle	eloquence	sweet	comfort	respect
long	demotivate	poor	illegal	squander
happy	overlook	inadequate	fragrant	disorder

1. **tranquil** _____
2. **scamper** _____
3. **distress** _____
4. **brief** _____
5. **hoard** _____
6. **conscientiousness** _____
7. **determined** _____
8. **rant** _____
9. **violate** _____
10. **rich** _____
11. **melancholy** _____
12. **observe** _____
13. **affection** _____
14. **malodorous** _____
15. **sour** _____
16. **complexity** _____
17. **sufficient** _____
18. **legal** _____
19. **structure** _____
20. **invigorate** _____

81. You May Be Right, But You Could Be Wrong

Instruction: Write the matching synonyms from the Word Bank underneath the words in bold.

Word Bank

misdeed	just	indictable	accurate	erroneous
equitable	upright	unlawful	virtuous	righteous
illicit	lawless	inaccurate	offence	fair
goodness	privilege	illegal	entitlement	faulty

Right	**Wrong**

82. Odd One Out

Instruction: Find which word is the odd one out. Cross it out.

1.	awful	dire	dreaded	please
2.	panic	chaos	fear	distraction
3.	gross	ugly	gorgeous	hideous
4.	sorrow	sadness	regret	joy
5.	plucky	vulnerable	mettlesome	dauntless
6.	wane	ebb	dwindle	eliminate
7.	give	abandon	leave	quit
8.	despair	hope	melancholy	desperation
9.	lethargy	inactivity	languor	energizing
10.	intertwined	brave	fearless	intrepid
11.	scared	quiver	shake	tremble
12.	grieve	grief	mourn	propriety
13.	blunder	blooper	bungle	bundle
14.	fatigue	excavate	weary	exhaustion
15.	hazardous	attention	danger	risky
16.	danger	peril	risk	courage
17.	dire	wrath	rage	ire
18.	defection	authorize	desertion	withdrawal
19.	bold	broken	valiant	valorous
20.	accomplish	achieve	attainment	attire

83. Synonyms

Instruction: Complete the synonym of the word in bold.

1. **precious**   v a __ __ __ __ l e

2. **hostility**   a n __ __ __ __ __ t y

3. **inquisitive**   q __ __ __ __ __ __ __ i n g

4. **candid**   s t __ __ __ __ __ __ __ __ __ __ __ d

5. **sovereignty**   a u __ __ __ __ m y

6. **approval**   a u __ __ __ __ __ __ __ __ __ o n

7. **soothe**   r e __ __ __ v e

8. **advantage**   b e __ __ __ __ t

9. **defeat**   f a __ __ __ r e

10. **eminent**   s u __ __ __ __ o r

11. **gratification**   s a __ __ __ __ __ __ __ __ o n

12. **leverage**   a d __ __ __ __ __ __ e

13. **preference**   f a __ __ __ r

14. **gain**   p __ __ __ i t

15. **help**   s u __ __ __ __ t

16. **authority**   j __ __ __ __ __ __ __ __ __ o n

17. **victory**   t r __ __ __ __ h

18. **delight**   p l __ __ __ __ __ e

19. **thrill**   e x __ __ __ __ __ __ n t

20. **horrible**   h o __ __ __ __ __ __ u s

84. Synonyms

Instruction: Choose the synonym of the word in bold.

1.	**unique**	simple	allowed	alike	special
2.	**vicious**	gentle	helpful	danger	cruel
3.	**precious**	necessary	usual	valuable	simple
4.	**bulky**	skinny	large	tender	sick
5.	**assist**	attend	apply	help	intend
6.	**criticize**	berate	prove	laud	enjoy
7.	**advocate**	predict	pronounce	support	determine
8.	**authorize**	verify	neglect	protect	empower
9.	**relegate**	prevaricate	promote	revitalize	downgrade
10.	**conquer**	surrender	descend	triumph	divide
11.	**enormous**	large	light	thin	small
12.	**instigate**	halt	cause	action	actual
13.	**amnesty**	pardon	obsolete	vice	doom
14.	**anxiety**	relief	harmony	unity	agitation
15.	**charity**	gift	theft	generosity	corruption
16.	**frosty**	sweltering	humid	arid	chilly
17.	**wondrous**	unsurprising	astounding	expected	bland
18.	**tyranny**	despotism	republican	conservative	democracy
19.	**flourish**	forest	thrive	threshold	flowers
20.	**pompous**	arrogant	advocate	artificial	aristocrat

85. Yes or No Game

Instructions: Write "Yes" in Column B if the words in Column A are antonyms. If they are NOT antonyms, write "No" then write an antonym for the first word. Several antonyms are possible.

Column A	Column B
1. excruciating – painful	
2. ostracize – expel	
3. prodigious – dread	
4. reluctant – eager	
5. erudite - brilliant	
6. outlandish - conventional	
7. apparent – obvious	
8. casual – planned	
9. precise – accurate	
10. sagacious – insightful	
11. reputable – notorious	
12. relevant – customary	
13. pessimism – optimism	
14. exciting – beautiful	
15. yummy – gross	
16. miniature – miniscule	
17. recent – ancient	
18. vice – virtue	
19. compulsory – obligatory	
20. steadfast – determined	

86. Rude and Polite

Instruction: Write the matching synonyms from the Word Bank underneath the words in bold.

Word Bank

gracious	gallant	unmannered	genteel	coarse
disrespectful	uncivil	courteous	mannerly	discourteous
civil	cultivated	impolite	impertinent	civilized
offensive	solicitous	Ill-mannered	boorish	well-behaved

Rude	**Polite**

87. Odd One Out

Instruction: Find which word is the odd one out. Cross it out.

1.	trust	belief	faith	suspect
2.	alter	change	amend	prescribe
3.	correctable	rechargeable	reversible	revocable
4.	entire	done	finished	complete
5.	docile	submissive	tamed	lame
6.	spend	frugal	sparing	thrifty
7.	anticipate	inflammation	await	expect
8.	facilitate	alleviate	easy-going	ease
9.	amend	assist	help	aid
10.	vacillate	subordinate	hesitate	fluctuate
11.	sloppy	lazy	slovenly	meticulous
12.	error	fault	mistake	regret
13.	hover	halt	arrest	hold
14.	plunder	loot	ransack	backpack
15.	exhort	inspire	urge	entourage
16.	conservative	affiliate	associate	consort
17.	modest	deceitful	humble	decent
18.	unbearable	intolerable	unendurable	endured
19.	abbreviated	mitigate	relieved	alleviated
20.	face	avoid	seek	confront

88. Antonym

Instruction: Complete the antonym of the word in bold.

1. **adult**   i m ___ ___ ___ ___ r e

2. **alleviate**   a g ___ ___ ___ ___ ___ t e

3. **attractive**   r e ___ ___ ___ ___ ___ v e

4. **disarrange**   a r ___ ___ ___ ___ e

5. **aggressive**   p e ___ ___ ___ ___ u l

6. **harmful**   h e ___ ___ ___ u l

7. **applaud**   c r ___ ___ ___ ___ s e

8. **concerned**   u n ___ ___ ___ ___ ___ ___ ___ e d

9. **together**   a p ___ ___ t

10. **atrocious**   w o ___ ___ ___ ___ ___ u l

11. **susceptible**   r e ___ ___ ___ ___ ___ n t

12. **closed**   a ___ ___ r

13. **calm**   a ___ g ___ y

14. **war**   p ___ ___ ___ e

15. **dead**   a n ___ ___ ___ ___ e d

16. **unlucky**   f o ___ ___ ___ ___ ___ t e

17. **lackadaisical**   e x ___ ___ ___ e d

18. **sobriety**   i n ___ ___ ___ ___ ___ ___ ___ ___ o n

19. **dauntless**   s c ___ ___ ___ d

20. **invincible**   v u ___ ___ ___ ___ ___ ___ l e

89. Synonym

Instruction: Write the matching synonym from the Word Bank on the blank.

Word Bank

gain	banality	giving	comply	quit
gaunt	exceptional	dismaying	startled	villainous
hasten	tawdry	query	mawkish	abundant
secretive	inspect	veritable	test	wonderful

1. obey _____

2. furtive _____

3. plentiful _____

4. scrawny _____

5. hurry _____

6. obtain _____

7. cliché _____

8. shocked _____

9. cease _____

10. inquiry _____

11. disturbing _____

12. shoddy _____

13. exam _____

14. generous _____

15. examine _____

16. nefarious _____

17. marvelous _____

18. sappy _____

19. outstanding _____

20. authentic _____

90. Dangerous and Safe

Instruction: Write the matching synonyms from the Word Bank underneath the words in bold.

Word Bank

wild	threatening	uninjured	menacing	vicious
savage	alright	risky	shielded	perilous
impregnable	harmless	precarious	defended	daredevil
prudent	reckless	cautious	unhurt	secure

Dangerous	**Safe**

91. Synonym

Instruction: Complete the synonym of the word in bold.

1. **pensive**   t h ___ ___ ___ ___ ___ ___ u l

2. **penitent**   r e ___ ___ ___ ___ ___ ___ u l

3. **cordial**   f r ___ ___ ___ ___ l y

4. **coarse**   r o ___ ___ h

5. **accumulate**   g a ___ ___ ___ r

6. **conquer**   d e ___ ___ ___ t

7. **uncommon**   u n ___ ___ ___ a l

8. **bliss**   h a ___ ___ ___ ___ ___ s s

9. **mischievous**   p l ___ ___ ___ ___ l

10. **assess**   e s ___ ___ ___ ___ ___ e

11. **brag**   b o ___ ___ t

12. **virtuous**   n ___ ___ ___ e

13. **cover up**   c o ___ ___ ___ ___ l

14. **rue**   r e ___ ___ ___ t

15. **peculiar**   s t ___ ___ ___ ___ e

16. **thrive**   f l ___ ___ ___ ___ s h

17. **disinfect**   s t ___ ___ ___ ___ ___ s e

18. **virtuous**   r i ___ ___ ___ ___ ___ u s

19. **resemble**   m i ___ ___ ___ r

20. **refrain**   f o ___ ___ ___ a r

92. Yes or No Game

Instructions: Write "Yes" in Column B if the words in Column A are antonyms. If they are NOT antonyms, write "No" then write an antonym for the first word. Several antonyms are possible.

Column A	Column B

Column A

1.   prompt – delayed

2.   candid – slow

3.   intrepid – wholesome

4.   hesitant – barren

5.   perspicuous – benevolent

6.   embrace – forefather

7.   meek – humble

8.   fragrant – stinky

9.   frail – fit

10. obscene – fictitious

11. decent – allude

12. despondent – hopeful

13. deserted – inhabited

14. aversion – fondness

15. impudence – desperation

16. jubilant – melancholic

17. defer – deft

18. cease – begin

19. cunning – prudent

20. persistent – crass

93. You Can Laugh All You Want, or Cry Me a River

Instruction: Write the matching synonyms from the Word Bank underneath the words in bold.

Word Bank

chuckle	weep	sob	chortle	giggle
wail	joke	smirk	jest	shout
shriek	cackle	whine	guffaw	mourn
mock	howl	titter	lament	whimper

Laugh	**Cry**

94. Synonym

Instruction: Write the matching synonym from the Word Bank on the blank.

Word Bank

hermetic	evaporate	classy	apathetic	solicit
irresolute	setback	align	uneducated	disclose
inertia	prolific	abundance	abandon	buoyant
chief	affable	habitual	empathetic	join

1. **vaporize** _____

2. **ask for** _____

3. **reversal** _____

4. **illiterate** _____

5. **inactivity** _____

6. **fertile** _____

7. **desert** _____

8. **principal** _____

9. **friendly** _____

10. **link** _____

11. **airtight** _____

12. **indifferent** _____

13. **elegant** _____

14. **usual** _____

15. **reveal** _____

16. **upbeat** _____

17. **plethora** _____

18. **compassionate** _____

19. **indecisive** _____

20. **line up** _____

95. Too Far or Very Near

Instruction: Write the matching synonyms from the Word Bank underneath the words in bold.

Word Bank

imminent	nearby	distant	remote	close
isolated	forthcoming	faraway	almost	removed
away	adjacent	outlying	godforsaken	further
afar	accessible	proximate	approaching	immediate

Far	**Near**

96. Synonym

Instruction: Complete the synonym of the word in bold.

1.   sterile   b a ___ ___ ___ n

2.   tender   c ___ ___ ___ ___ g

3.   contemplate   c o ___ ___ ___ ___ e r

4.   resentment   b i t ___ ___ ___ ___ ___ s s

5.   amend   r e ___ ___ ___ e

6.   disclosure   r e v ___ ___ ___ ___ ___ o n

7.   expel   b a ___ ___ ___ h

8.   berate   c e ___ ___ ___ ___ e

9.   imbecility   s ___ ___ ___ ___ ___ ___ t y

10. rustic   r ___ ___ ___ l

11. collusion   a g ___ ___ ___ ___ ___ n t

12. invalidate   n e ___ ___ ___ e

13. peril   d ___ ___ ___ ___ r

14. vindictive   v ___ ___ ___ ___ ___ ___ u l

15. hostility   e n ___ ___ t y

16. reject   d i s ___ ___ ___ ___ ___ v e

17. remorse   r ___ ___ ___ e t

18. weary   f a ___ ___ ___ ___ e d

19. shake   t r ___ ___ ___ ___ e

20. salient   i m ___ ___ ___ ___ ___ n t

97. Short and Tall

Instruction: Write the matching synonyms from the Word Bank underneath the words in bold.

Word Bank

tiny	squat	brief	towering	colossal
elevated	fleeting	teeny	altitudinous	wee
petite	diminutive	monstrous	compact	giant
steep	lofty	gigantic	high	miniscule

Short	**Tall**

98. Yes or No Game

Instructions: Write "Yes" in Column B if the words in Column A are antonyms. If they are NOT antonyms, write "No" then write an antonym for the first word. Several antonyms are possible.

Column A	Column B
1. amicable – hearten	
2. ample – enough	
3. meager – sufficient	
4. baleful – beneficent	
5. deference – courteous	
6. dormant – active	
7. dubious – confident	
8. unprecedented – common	
9. deception – falsehood	
10. innumerable – countable	
11. immeasurable – delayed	
12. perpetual – constant	
13. evoke – elicit	
14. flimsy – powerful	
15. garish – gaudy	
16. indict – advocate	
17. untried – ancient	
18. veracity – misinformation	
19. latent – obvious	
20. reparation - restitution	

99. Synonym

Instruction: Write the matching synonym from the Word Bank on the blank.

Word Bank

fragile	apprise	consensus	treason	loyal
amiable	lucent	ravaged	ephemeral	filthy
anonymous	extravagant	hinder	relish	vague
sage	delirious	squander	abrogate	submissive

1. short-lived _____

2. impede _____

3. destroyed _____

4. inform _____

5. dirty _____

6. spendthrift _____

7. devoted _____

8. enjoy _____

9. unknown _____

10. agreement _____

11. delicate _____

12. luminous _____

13. unclear _____

14. waste _____

15. friendly _____

16. repeal _____

17. betrayal _____

18. hallucinating _____

19. servile _____

20. wise _____

100. Remember Me or Forget All About Me

Instruction: Write the matching synonyms from the Word Bank underneath the words in bold.

Word Bank

recall	recollect	place	learn	ignore
commemorate	neglect	remind	overlook	memorize
unlearn	erase	reminisce	blank	elude
retrieve	neglect	recapture	escape	misremember

Remember	**Forget**

Answer Key

1. 1.mend 2.foe 3.dislike 4.frown 5.fresh 6.dangerous 7.finish 8.future 9.laugh 10.easy 11.worse 12.unknown 13.dead 14.leave 15.unstable 16.end 17.doubt 18.colourful 19.tiny 20.same

2. Happy (cheery, gleeful, merry, sunny, upbeat, grinning, beaming, jolly, buoyant, contented)
   Sad (sorrowful, miserable, depressed, blue, down, gloomy, glum, woeful, forlorn, woebegone)

3. 1.away 2.copious 3.greatest 4.warped 5.receive 6.disclose 7.transparent 8.tranquil 9.friendly 10.careful 11.omit 12.correct 13.very important 14.delicious 15.puzzling 16.solidarity 17.repay 18.area 19.bypass 20.frank

4. 1.yes 2.no 3.yes 4.yes 5.no 6.yes 7.no 8.no 9.no 10.yes 11.yes 12.no 13.yes 14.no 15.no 16.yes 17.yes 18.yes 19.yes 20.no

5. Strong (athletic, powerful, forceful, tough, solid, fit, firm, brawny, redoubtable, stout)
   Weak (fragile, sick, delicate, fatigued, infirm, spent, debilitated, feeble, rickety, flimsy)

6. 1.occur 2.deny 3.rough 4.worth 5.ancient 6.silent 7.carpet 8.enquire 9.author 10.blend 11.liberty 12.monotony 13.insert 14.sugary 15.tiny 16.unwell 17.deceive 18.courageous 19.honesty 20.continue

7. Lots (plenty, many, tons, heaps, myriad, copious, dozens, several, piles, abundant)
   Few (meager, lean, infrequent, sparse, rare, scarce, slight, scant, paltry, little)

8. 1.guilty 2.bold 3.complicated 4.extravagance 5.sharp 6.sterile 7.quiet 8.hazardous 9.discourteous 10.accurate 11.energetic 12.treacherous 13.question 14.aimlessness 15.pull 16.enemy 17.never 18.occupied 19.obscure 20.rare

9. 1.reject 2.adjust 3.achieve 4.adolescent 5.stray 6.bare 7.draught 8.shrink 9.awful
10.sob 11.divine 12.above 13.smooth 14.once 15.scream 16.scrawny 17.rigid 18.sickly
19.filled 20.seldom

10. Beautiful (comely, alluring, exquisite, attractive, pleasant, dazzling, enthralling,
stunning, gorgeous, lovely)
Ugly (hideous, unsightly, ghastly, nasty, repellent, repulsive, deformed, awful,
grotesque, disgusting)

11. 1.absolve 2.contrast 3.fluctuate 4.generate 5.mediate 6.traumatic 7.beneficial 8.valid
9.mandatory 10.dilemma 11.perception 12.scrutiny 13.elude 14.infamous
15.alternative 16.mistake 17.evaluate 18.derive 19.mortify 20.sabotage

12. 1.trust 2.voracious 3.pleasure 4.diligent 5.reject 6.significant 7.empty 8.pleasant
9.boast 10.grant 11.fast 12.sleepy 13.drowsy 14.tidy 15.mushy 16.upset 17.masculine
18.malicious 19.teenager 20.mature

13. Forbid (restrain, ban, preclude, veto, block, sanction, disallow, prohibit, interdict,
outlaw, proscribe)
Permit (enjoin, authorize, permit, approve, entitle, grant, let, empower, allow)

14. 1.deduct 2.flourish 3.deficient 4.immune 5.enthusiastic 6.converge 7.leave 8.begin
9. tranquility 10.carnivore 11.implicit 12.diurnal 13.inaccurate 14.formidable
15.inclusive 16.protagnonist 17.climb 18.agitation 19.virtuoso 20.outgoing

15. 1.modest 2.resilient 3.graceful 4.repel 5.bearded 6.leave 7.outgoing 8.accept 9.plain
10.luxury 11.give 12.present 13.offense 14.deteriorate 15.abandon 16.narrow 17.safe
18.vanish 19.prevent 20.useless

16. 1.modest 2.deafening 3.contemporary 4.wealthy 5.cynic 6.untruth 7.bucket 8.wait
9.unhappy 10.protect 11.quick-witted 12.strong 13.vigilant 14.revelation 15.brawl
16.organize 17.divert 18.command 19.grasp 20.accept

17. Smart (clever, savvy, perceptive, brainy, alert, sharp, bright, intelligent, genius, brilliant)
    Stupid (ignorant, foolish, ludicrous, thick, dumb, mindless, brainless, imbecile, silly, dummy)

18. 1.yes 2.no 3.no 4.no 5.no 6.no 7.no 8.yes 9.no 10.yes 11.yes 12.no 13.yes 14.yes 15.no 16.no 17.yes 18.yes 19.no 20.no

19. 1.hate 2.bellitle 3.forgive 4.brother 5.allow 6.immorality 7.push 8.desire 9.present 10.classroom 11.error 12.prediction 13.liability 14.letter 15.ancient 16.enthusiastic 17.skepticism 18.promptness 19.attic 20.remorse

20. Big (substantial, huge, great, enormous, mighty, gigantic, colossal, stupendous, massive, jumbo)
    Small (diminutive, petite, tiny, slight, compact, insignificant, miniature, minuscule, microscopic, baby)

21. 1.irrelevant 2.empty 3.satisfied 4.temporary 5.sparse 6.original 7.trivial 8.true 9.demand 10.white 11.increase 12.vacant 13.merciful 14.stay 15.against 16.con 17.concrete 18.specific 19.night 20.melt

22. 1.include 2.purchase 3.fright 4.seat 5.delayed 6.inner 7.confess 8.additional 9.carry 10.seize 11.terror 12.come 13.actual 14.movement 15.ignore 16.adore 17.flunk 18.prepared 19.greatest 20.alike

23. Clean (unsoiled, washed, tidy, pure, spotless, scrubbed, unstained, sanitary, hygienic, cleansed)
    Dirty (filthy, grimy, mucky, nasty, greasy, contaminated, icky, stained, foul, obscene)

24. 1.uphill 2.take-off 3.theory 4.asset 5.deport 6.allegiance 7.exit 8.land 9.different 10.absence 11.import 12.liquid 13.safety 14.primary 15.belief 16.inferior 17.anonymous 18.departure 19.proof 20.proximity

25.   1.split 2.plain 3.triumph 4.holiday 5.belongings 6.distress 7.cease 8.brutality 9.elderly
       10.ballot 11.obtain 12.country 13.learn 14.current 15.quest 16.youthful 17.malevolent
       18.inform 19.movie 20.incorrect

26.   Similar (comparable, equivalent, matching, akin, alike, related, homogeneous,
       resembling, close, analogous)
       Different (discrete, disparate, individual, dissimilar, incompatible, unusual, contrasting,
              distinct, inconsistent, diverse)

27.   1.correct 2.humid 3.there 4.solid 5.maximum 6.nobody 7.yesterday 8.absent 9.center
       10.approximately 11.alive 12.outrageous 13.divide 14.heaven 15.bottom 16.servant
       17.public 18.native 19.worst 20.learn

28.   1.sickness 2.dullness 3.jeopardy 4.sometimes 5.stink 6.boring 7.endangered 8.suffering
       9.cautious 10.eager 11.forest 12.vindictive 13.scene 14.direct 15.loyalty 16.joy
       17.insomnia 18.demonstrate 19.eradicate 20.forcefully

29.   Fresh (new, natural, unspoiled, pristine, original, pure, unprocessed, clean,
       unpreserved, uncured)
       Stale (old, rotten, spoiled, off, hardened, rancid, decayed, dry, musty, timeworn)

30.   1.outside 2.clean 3.book 4.wound 5.heal 6.musty 7.derive 8.apart 9.neighbor
       10.finish 11.treacherous 12.monochrome 13.unicorn 14.superb 15.sunrise
       16.inaugurate 17.prudent 18.proud 19.outburst 20.wreck

31.   1.yes 2.no 3.yes 4.no 5.no 6.yes 7.yes 8.yes 9.no 10.yes 11.no 12.no 13.no 14.no 15.no
       16.no 17.yes 18.yes 19.yes 20.yes

32.   Try (test, attempt, seek, strive, aspire, effort, taste, check, experiment, endeavor)
       Quit (retire, withdraw, leave, abandon, cease, drop, resign, left, desert, discontinue)

33.   1.nice 2.complicated 3.pleased 4.loud 5.petite 6.woman 7.unhappy 8.enormous

9.fascinating 10.unusual 11.baggy 12.scorching 13.waste 14.absurd 15.huge 16.careful 17.disagree 18.brave 19.succeed 20.annoy

34. 1.die 2.partial 3.winter 4.clean 5.last 6.laugh 7.build 8.healthy 9.common 10.untrustworthy 11.destroy 12.soft 13.normal 14.fairness 15.peace 16.skinny 17.woman 18.youthful 19.close 20.country

35. Problem (trouble, issue, challenge, difficulty, complication, worry, nuisance, obstacle, concern, predicament)
     Solution (result, answer, determination, finding, solving, key, explication, conclusion, resolution, explanation)

36. 1.nasty 2.thankful 3.accurate 4.sell 5.break 6.among 7.steel 8.dice 9.recede 10.friendly 11.fiction 12.commence 13.missile 14.shift 15.deluxe 16.condition 17.style 18.mushroom 19.heat 20.shiver

37. 1.distant 2.relative 3.pleasant 4.imposter 5.pull 6.cautious 7.spoils 8.suggest 9.extend 10.humble 11.brave 12.helpful 13.settle 14.deceive 15.dwell 16.meeting 17.tailored 18.distant 19.careless 20.blaze

38. Luck (fortune, chance, fate, destiny, serendipity, fortuity, providence, windfall, happenstance, fluke)
     Misfortune (calamity, mishap, misery, catastrophe, tribulation, disaster, difficulty, hardship, tragedy, setback)

39. 1.neglect 2.sink 3.delight 4.master 5.common 6.calm 7.cowardice 8.compassionate 9.stupid 10.peace 11.guilty 12.obvious 13.boastful 14.interesting 15.expand 16.sweet 17.darkness 18.punish 19.initial 20.reject

40. 1.weak 2.hide 3.gather 4.adversity 5.brute 6.attentive 7.dissipate 8.kind 9.agitate 10.follow 11.result 12.fake 13.shortage 14.talk 15.emit 16.impure 17.brief 18.mercy 19.display 20.fair

41. Loud (noisy, deafening, boisterous, roaring, rowdy, blaring, clamorous, ear-splitting, thunderous, resounding)
     Quiet (peace, tranquil, placid, subdued, pacify, still, hush, serene, soundless, silent)

42. 1.no 2.yes 3.yes 4.yes 5.no 6.yes 7.yes 8.no 9.yes 10.no 11.yes 12.no 13.no 14.yes 15.yes 16.yes 17.yes 18.yes 19.no 20.yes

43. 1.conflict 2.guest 3.upper 4.friendship 5.darling 6.disregard 7.smooth 8.misuse 9.receive 10.ribbon 11.plea 12.announce 13.unity 14.great 15.awake 16.traffic 17.povery 18.defeat 19.gross 20.gradual

44. 1.wealth 2.force 3.melody 4.watch 5.help 6.jump 7.prize 8.dazzling 9.careful 10.party 11.touch 12.finish 13.cash 14.shiny 15.gloomy 16.cramped 17.crunchy 18.wonder 19.bathe 20.success

45. Guilty (ashamed, responsible, culpable, sinful, blamable, convicted, criminal, repentant, remorseful, contrite)
     Innocent (untainted, pure, naive, blameless, chaste, faultless, inoffensive, vindicated, acquitted, exonerated)

46. 1.mother 2.intellect 3.hit 4.brother 5.older 6.few 7.answer 8.short 9.wife 10.hopeful 11.chaos 12.asleep 13.cold 14.give up 15.changeable 16.earier 17.devil 18.adults 19.negative 20.none

47. 1.emergency 2.known 3.view 4.genuine 5.kind 6.stimulating 7.sweet 8.train 9.manage 10.terrible 11.cook 12.exaggerate 13.marvel 14.destroy 15.hit 16.wet 17.return 18.belittle 19.evening 20.nothing

48. 1.host 2.detailed 3.finite 4.reflection 5.incomparable 6.wicked 7.compound 8.fright 9.squeak 10.diminutive 11.neutral 12.default 13.rigid 14.stretch 15.determined 16.mundane 17.advertize 18.fragile 19.irrelevant 20.impediment

49. 1.soft 2.find 3.above 4.warm 5.tall 6.organized 7.light 8.early 9.full 10.far 11.dry 12.enormous 13.far 14.light 15.narrow 16.near 17.slow 18.full 19.dumb 20.entrance

50. Friend (buddy, companion, ally, comrade, mate, pal, associate, fellow, partner, supporter)
Foe (enemy, opponent, rival, attacker, competitor, antagonist, adversary, challenger, arch-enemy, disputant)

51. 1.no 2.yes 3.no 4.yes 5.yes 6.yes 7.no 8.yes 9.yes 10.no 11.no 12.no 13.no 14.no 15.yes 16.yes 17.yes 18.yes 19.yes 20.yes

52. 1.deny 2.past 3.contemporary 4.virtue 5.obligatory 6.optional 7.dissent 8.caring 9.miserable 10.downcast 11.celebrate 12.few 13.clever 14.goodwill 15.obvious 16.confirm 17.slow 18.friendly 19.false 20.precise

53. 1.contract 2.conflict 3.answer 4.teach 5.right 6.sea 7.dessert 8.leave 9.forget 10.amulet 11.question 12.petrified 13.dishonest 14.abnormal 15.scarce 16.infamous 17.philanthropy 18.culpability 19.commemoration 20.aside

54. 1.clumsy 2.defame 3.petrified 4.assault 5.plaudit 6.bountiful 7.answer 8.allegation 9.detest 10.loyal 11.abominable 12.acquit 13.unbeliever 14.laudable 15.retort 16.munificence 17.tear 18.ask 19.slander 20.unconventional

55. Hide (conceal, cover, mask, shield, shroud, camouflage, envelop, secret, disguise, bury)
Seek (look for, scout, browse, hunt, pursue, desire, quest, search, root out, forage)

56. 1.arrogant 2.bless 3.serious 4.gather 5.native 6.feeble 7.shrink 8.innocent 9.repair 10.forgiving 11.lurch 12.abundant 13.dispatcher 14.hasten 15.monumental 16.insignificant 17.crazy 18.scarce 19.careful 20.associate

57.   1.yes 2.no 3.yes 4.no 5.no 6.yes 7.yes 8.no 9.no 10.yes 11.no 12.yes 13.yes 14.no 15.no 16.no 17.yes 18.yes 19.yes 20.yes

58.   High (towering, elevated, tall, soaring, upper, lifted, above, escalated, heightened, lofty)
       Low (despicable, miserable, inferior, abject, blue, gloomy, down, downcast, base, sunken)

59.   1.outmoded 2.placate 3.affable 4.vicious 5.palliate 6.animosity 7.appropriate 8.addition 9.antipathy 10.lure 11.affinity 12.excuse 13.antiquated 14.disagreeable 15.wheedle 16. incognito 17.repel 18.languid 19.imbue 20.resist

60.   1.disrespect 2.break 3.abbreviate 4.conclude 5.frustrate 6.repair 7.unrestraint 8.crude 9.begin 10.energy 11.increase 12.notice 13.cautious 14.heartless 15.acquire 16.bold 17.inattentive 18.languish 19.diminish 20.temperamental

61.   Intense (ardent, profound, strong, rich, resonant, serious, extensive, immeasurable, earnest, great)
       Shallow (surface, superficial, foolish, unimportant, trivial, petty, glib, silly, flimsy, frivolous)

62.   1.yes 2.yes 3.yes 4.yes 5.yes 6.no 7.yes 8.yes 9.no 10.no 11.no 12.yes 13.yes 14.no 15.yes 16.no 17.no 18.yes 19.yes 20.no

63.   1.apex 2.capricious 3.elated 4.crude 5.apropos 6.grueling 7.remorseful 8.squabble 9.elongate 10.eloquent 11.augur 12.authentic 13.parsimonious 14.poise 15.apprentice 16.determined 17.hackneyed 18.tyrannical 19.banish 20.amazing

64.   1.amateur 2.sharp 3.calm 4.hope 5.attest 6.supply 7.agree 8.reproduce 9.stale 10.frown 11.hasty 12.disorder 13.fail 14.crawl 15.fraternity 16.flavored 17.blemished 18.chomp 19.disagree 20.reproduction

65.   1.anger 2.pretentious 3.disaster 4.wince 5.shallow 6.streak 7.sparkle 8.correct
        9.influence 10.terminate 11.tenacity 12.perplex 13.unnecessary 14.deceitful
        15.venture 16.impudent 17.occult 18.tedious 19.welfare 20.futile

66.   Dark (gloomy, black, night, obscure, grim, dismal, shady, dreary, dim, nightfall)
        Light (illumination, pale, brightness, shine, radiant, bright, glow, clear, fair, lamp)

67.   1.delay 2.retain 3.assert 4.tractable 5.agreeable 6.constructive 7.love 8.accept
        9.eradicate 10.misunderstand 11.conquer 12.fake 13.cruelty 14.benevolence
        15.superior 16.purify 17.indifferent 18.restriction 19.tardy 20.strong

68.   1.chewy 2.furry 3.music 4.write 5.lame 6.curious 7.inauspicious 8.adjective 9.chant
        10.pessimism 11.center 12.retire 13.hesitation 14.figurative 15.bachelor 16.insane
        17.intestine 18.adhesion 19.fully 20.bloated

69.   1.no 2.yes 3.yes 4.yes 5.yes 6.no 7.no 8.no 9.yes 10.yes 11.yes 12.yes 13.no 14.yes
        15.yes 16.yes 17.no 18.no 19.no 20.no

70.   1.confiscate 2.adulation 3.toxic 4.scorn 5.benevolent 6.mischievous
        7.ameliorate 8.deteriorate 9.limited 10.decrease 11.gloomy 12.great 13.grow 14.awe
        15.immaculate 16.unpleasant 17.principal 18.paradox 19.invulnerable 20.filthy

71.   Open (candid, clear, honest, free, unlock, start, begin, initiate, commence, direct)
        Close (suspend, finalize, finish, end, terminate, complete, conclude, shut, stop, cease)

72.   1.comfort 2.success 3.scarcity 4.disappoint 5.punctual 6.obsolete 7.ignite 8.cultivate
        9.accentuate 10.receive 11.deduct 12.gradual 13.antiquated 14.manual 15.unique
        16.diverse 17.purposeful 18.present 19.irregular 20.refute

73.   1.yes 2.no 3.no 4.yes 5.yes 6.yes 7.yes 8.yes 9.no 10.no 11.no 12.no 13.no 14.no 15.yes
        16.yes 17.yes 18.yes 19.yes 20.no

74. Vacant (empty, blank, void, free, deserted, vacuous, uninhabited, available, abandoned, devoid)
Occupied (busy, engaged, preoccupied, employed, taken, full, working, inhabited, active, involved)

75. 1.deception 2.sympathy 3.garnish 4.lively 5.skillful 6.alluring 7.conversant 8.anguish 9.destitute 10.demolition 11.construct 12.direct 13.secret 14.unconventional 15.aversion 16.gaiety 17.faithful 18.friendly 19.honored 20.instructive

76. 1.guilt 2.triumph 3.lively 4.laughter 5.hatred 6.reckless 7.misdeed 8.wild 9.satisfy 10.impeach 11.pleasant 12.valuable 13.rumor 14.haste 15.explain 16.sell 17.refined 18.forbid 19.relaxed 20.blunt

77. New (original, current, contemporary, novel, unprecedented, fresh, avant-garde, unknown, modern)
Old (former, remote, shabby, mature, bygone, aged, worn, medieval, antique, archaic, past)

78. 1.yes 2.no 3.no 4.no 5.no 6.yes 7.yes 8.yes 9.no 10.no 11.yes 12.yes 13.no 14.yes 15.no 16.yes 17.yes 18.yes 19.no 20.no

79. 1.substantial 2.request 3.giggle 4.stroll 5.glimpse 6.affection 7.sorrowful 8.pleasing 9.refined 10.extraordinary 11.teeny 12.packed 13.considerate 14.funny 15.humorous 16.witty 17.jocund 18.amble 19.stunning 20.admiration

80. 1.disturbed 2.dawdle 3.comfort 4.long 5.squander 6.carelessness 7.discouraged 8.eloquence 9.respect 10.poor 11.happy 12.overlook 13.antipathy 14.fragrant 15.sweet 16.simplicity 17.inadequate 18.illegal 19.disorder 20.demotivate

81. Right (just, accurate, equitable, upright, virtuous, righteous, fair, goodness, privilege, entitlement)
Wrong (misdeed, indictable, erroneous, unlawful, illicit, lawless, inaccurate, offence, illegal, faulty)

82.   1.please 2.distraction 3.gorgeous 4.joy 5.vulnerable 6.eliminate 7.give 8.hope 9.energizing 10.intertwined 11.scared 12.propriety 13.bundle 14.excavate 15.attention 16.courage 17.dire 18.authorize 19.broken 20.attire

83.   1.valuable 2.animosity 3.questioning 4.straightforward 5.autonomy 6.authorization 7.relieve 8.benefit 9.failure 10.superior 11.satisfaction 12.advantage 13.favor 14.profit 15.support 16.jursidiction 17.triumph 18.pleasure 19.excitement 20.horrendous

84.   1.special 2.cruel 3.valuable 4.large 5.help 6.berate 7.support 8.empower 9.downgrade 10.triumph 11.large 12.cause 13.pardon 14.agitation 15.generosity 16.chilly 17.astounding 18.despotism 19.thrive 20.arrogant

85.   1.no 2.no 3.no 4.yes 5.no 6.yes 7.no 8.yes 9.no 10.no 11.yes 12.no 13.yes 14.no 15.yes 16.no 17.yes 18.yes 19.no 20.no

86.   Rude (unmannered, coarse, disrespectful, uncivil, discourteous, impolite, impertinent, offensive, ill-mannered, boorish)
    Polite (gracious, gallant, genteel, civil, courteous, cultivated, civilized, mannerly, solicitous, well-behaved)

87.   1.suspect 2.prescribe 3.rechargeable 4.entire 5.lame 6.spend 7.inflammation 8.easygoing 9.amend 10.subordinate 11.meticulous 12.regret 13.hover 14.backpack 15.entourage 16.conservative 17.deceitful 18.endured 19.abbreviated 20.avoid

88.   1.immature 2.aggravate 3.repulsive 4.arrange 5.peaceful 6.helpful 7.criticize 8.unconcerned 9.apart 10.wonderful 11.resistant 12.ajar 13.angry 14.peace 15.animated 16.fortunate 17.excited 18.intoxication 19.scared 20.vulnerable

89.   1.comply 2.secretive 3.abundant 4.gaunt 5.hasten 6.gain 7.banality 8.startled 9.quit 10.query 11.dismaying 12.tawdry 13.test 14.giving 15.inspect 16.villainous 17.wonderful 18.mawkish 19.exceptional 20.veritable

90. Dangerous (wild, threatening, menacing, vicious, savage, risky, perilous, daredevil, reckless, precarious)
    Safe (uninjured, alright, shielded, impregnable, harmless, defended, prudent, cautious, unhurt, secure)

91. 1.thoughtful 2.remorseful 3.friendly 4.rough 5.gather 6.defeat 7.unusual 8.happiness 9.playful 10.estimate 11.boast 12.noble 13.conceal 14.regret 15.strange 16.flourish 17. sterilize 18.righteous 19.mirror 20.forbear

92. 1.yes 2.no 3.no 4.no 5.no 6.no 7.no 8.yes 9.yes 10.no 11.no 12.yes 13.yes 14.yes 15.no 16.yes 17.no 18.yes 19.no 20.no

93. Laugh (chuckle, chortle, giggle, joke, smirk, jest, cackle, guffaw, mock, titter)
    Cry (weep, sob, wail, shout, shriek, whine, mourn, lament, whimper, howl)

94. 1.evaporate 2.solicit 3.setback 4.uneducated 5.inertia 6.prolific 7.abandon 8.chief 9.affable 10.join 11.hermetic 12.apathetic 13.classy 14.habitual 15.disclose 16.buyoant 17.abundance 18.empathetic 19.irresolute 20.align

95. Far (distant, remote, isolated, faraway, removed, away, outlying, godforsaken, afar, further)
    Near (imminent, nearby, close, almost, forthcoming, adjacent, accessible, proximate, approaching, immediate)

96. 1.barren 2.caring 3.consider 4.bitterness 5.revise 6.revelation 7.banish 8.censure 9.stupidity 10.rural 11.agreement 12.negate 13.danger 14.vengeful 15.enmity 16.disapprove 17.regret 18.fatigued 19.tremble 20.important

97. Short (tiny, squat, miniscule, brief, fleeting, teeny, wee, petite, diminutive, compact)
    Tall (towering, colossal, elevated, altitudinous, monstrous, giant, steep, lofty, gigantic, high)

98.   1.no 2.no 3.yes 4.yes 5.no 6.yes 7.yes 8.yes 9.no 10.yes 11.no 12.no 13.no 14.yes 15.no
        16.yes 17.no 18.yes 19.yes 20.no

99.   1.ephemeral 2.hinder 3.ravaged 4.apprise 5.filthy 6.extravagant 7.loyal 8.relish
        9.anonymous 10.consensus 11.fragile 12.lucent 13.vague 14.squander 15.amiable
        16.abrogate 17.treason 18.delirious 19.submissive 20.sage

100.   Remember (recall, recollect, place, learn, commemorate, remind, memorize, reminisce,
                retrieve, recapture)
        Forget (ignore, neglect, overlook, unlearn, erase, blank, elude, neglect, escape,
                misremember)

Made in the USA
Las Vegas, NV
02 December 2024

13207859R00066